PRO WRESTLING LEGENDS

CHELSEA HOUSE PUBLISHERS

Pro Wrestling's Greatest Matches

Matt Hunter

Chelsea House Publishers
Philadelphia

Produced by Chestnut Productions and Choptank Syndicate, Inc.
Editor and Picture Researcher: Mary Hull
Design and Production: Lisa Hochstein

CHELSEA HOUSE PUBLISHERS

Editor in Chief: Sally Cheney
Associate Editor in Chief: Kim Shinners
Production Manager: Pamela Loos
Art Director: Sara Davis
Director of Photography: Judy L. Hasday

Cover Photos: Sports Action
            and Jeff Eisenberg Sports Photography

The Chelsea House World Wide Web site
address is http://www.chelseahouse.com

First Printing

1 3 5 7 9 8 6 4 2

Library of Congress Cataloging-in-Publication Data

Hunter, Matt.
    Pro wrestling's greatest matches / Matt Hunter.
       p. cm. — (Pro wrestling legends)
    Includes bibliographical references (p.) and index.
    ISBN 0–7910–6459–X (alk. paper) — ISBN 0–7910–6460–3 (pbk. : alk. paper)
       1. Wrestling—History—Juvenile literature. [1. Wrestling—History.] I. Title. II. Series.

GV1195.3 H86 2001
796.812'09732—dc21
[B]
                                                        00–069411

Contents

The evening of April 11, 1987, was one of the most emotional nights ever in professional wrestling history. The occasion was the second day of the two-day Jim Crockett Sr. Memorial Cup tag team championship hosted by the National Wrestling Alliance (NWA) in Baltimore. A $1 million prize was at stake.

In the final match of the tournament, three-time NWA World heavyweight champion "American Dream" Dusty Rhodes and two-time NWA World tag team champion and then-U.S. heavyweight champion Nikita Koloff squared off against Arn Anderson and Tully Blanchard, a top team that later won the NWA World tag team title.

Koloff's U.S. championship was a notable one. He captured the belt on August 17, 1986, from Terry Allen (better known as Magnum T.A.) in the final match of a memorable best-of-seven series for the championship. Two months after losing the title to Koloff, Magnum crashed his Porsche into a utility pole. The charismatic man deemed a future world champion was paralyzed. He required extensive surgery and physical therapy. Doctors said he'd never walk again.

So when the spotlight in the darkened Baltimore Arena shone on the aisle connecting the dressing room to the ring

"American Dream" Dusty Rhodes, known for his longstanding feud with Ric Flair in the NWA, teamed with Nikita Koloff to win the Jim Crockett Sr. Memorial Cup tag team championship.

What makes wrestling great is the excitement generated by competition, the matching of wits and skills, and the fact that you never know what might happen.

and highlighted Magnum T.A., his arm in a sling, walking precariously and painfully—but walking!—to the ring, the crowd in the sold-out arena rose to their feet. The applause seemed as if it would never end. Fans were weeping as Magnum made his way to ringside and hugged Nikita, his former enemy, and Dusty, his life-long friend.

Rhodes and Koloff captured the million-dollar prize that night, but their match against

Blanchard and Anderson could hardly be called a marvel of technical excellence. As fans left the Baltimore Arena, though, they had no doubt in their minds: They had just witnessed a great match. The emotional context of the evening had transformed the bout from something rather ordinary into something truly extraordinary.

Of course, an emotion-filled night like this comes along once in a wrestling lifetime, but there are also many other things that can elevate a match into something truly great.

One fan may prefer a pure scientific battle of wits and sheer athleticism, a contest in which subtle mat wrestling means the difference between victory or defeat. Another fan may prefer an ultraviolent war in which bodies are hurled from atop steel cages, smashed through wooden tables, and carried away on stretchers.

While there are probably hundreds—if not thousands—of matches that could legitimately be termed "great," this volume could never provide a comprehensive overview of every great match in wrestling history.

What we have done, however, is examine hundreds of important matches, past and present, to find great matches in five categories: world title matches, other championship matches involving singles titles, grudge matches, tag team matches, and specialty matches.

The matches that are presented in this volume are great for many reasons, as you will see, but they all share one common quality: each is an example of the heights of excellence and competitive passion that make pro wrestling truly one of the greatest sports in the world.

GREAT WORLD TITLE MATCHES

They are wrestling's biggest prizes: the solo world championships that guarantee a place in pro wrestling history for the select few who manage to capture them.

Many organizations have said that their top titles are world championships, but there are currently only two organizations in the United States that can claim world championship status with any validity: the World Wrestling Federation (WWF) and World Championship Wrestling (WCW).

Until the mid-1990s, when the National Wrestling Alliance (NWA) slipped from being the dominant promotion to a far smaller regional entity, the NWA championship title was viewed as one of the biggest prizes in the sport. The NWA title stretches back officially to 1948.

World title matches are always an occasion for the fans to sit up and take notice. Here are 10 of the very best of the past 20 years.

RIC FLAIR vs. HARLEY RACE
(November 24, 1983)

On June 10, 1983, Harley Race made wrestling history when he defeated "Nature Boy" Ric Flair to capture his unprecedented seventh NWA World heavyweight title. The win

---

Ric Flair defeated legendary longtime NWA champion Harley Race for the federation's world title at Starrcade '83, launching his own long and storied NWA career in the process.

put Race one reign ahead of the legendary Lou Thesz, who held the NWA belt six times.

Yet Flair, who had worn the belt since September 17, 1981, was not about to let Race enjoy the spotlight for long.

The location was Greensboro, North Carolina on November 24, 1983, and the occasion was Starrcade '83. A crowd of 15,447 was on hand in the Greensboro Coliseum to watch the match between Flair and Race, with another 30,000 fans tuning in via closed-circuit television. Flair came into the match a slight favorite, and he didn't disappoint.

When a bloodied Flair left the ring, he was holding the NWA World championship belt high for all the fans to see. It was the first time ever that the NWA World title had changed hands inside a steel cage.

HULK HOGAN vs. THE IRON SHEIK (January 23, 1984)

There was enormous controversy coming into this match. The Iron Sheik had ended Bob Backlund's four-year WWF World title reign about a month earlier, on December 26, 1983. Backlund had hoped to wrestle in the rematch, but a back injury prevented him from doing so. Enter Hulk Hogan, who had been wrestling in the American Wrestling Association (AWA) just weeks earlier. When Hogan got the title match, the other WWF wrestlers were outraged.

Nevertheless, it was Hogan who entered the Madison Square Garden ring to square off against the Sheik. The match was all Hogan. A bit more than five minutes into the match, Hogan hurled Sheik into the ropes. Sheik rebounded. Hogan met Sheik with a big boot to the face. Sheik collapsed. Hogan hurled himself against the ropes and delivered a legdrop that led to a three-count victory.

At the 5:40 mark, a new WWF World champion was crowned. Hulkamania was born, and it was a phenomenon that carried Hogan to a four-year title reign (and four more WWF reigns thereafter) and the WWF to incredible heights of popularity in the mid-1980s.

KERRY VON ERICH vs. RIC FLAIR
(May 6, 1984)

Few world title matches have ever been wrestled with the emotional context of this incredible NWA World title contest. On February 10, 1984, David Von Erich died in his sleep in a hotel room in Tokyo, Japan. David was beloved throughout the sport, and viewed by most experts as a future NWA champion.

David's brother, Kerry, entered the ring on May 6, 1984, at Texas Stadium in front of more than 43,000 fans. If the home field advantage has any meaning in wrestling, Ric Flair didn't have a chance: There wasn't a fan on hand who didn't want to see Kerry win the belt for David.

The match was a remarkably even contest that saw each man score many near-falls. Hearts jumped when it appeared as if Flair would retain the title, then they soared as Von Erich scored the pinfall. Fans cried as Kerry took the belt not only for himself, but for David and all of Texas.

HULK HOGAN vs. ANDRE THE GIANT
(March 29, 1987)

The main event of WrestleMania III was one of the most anticipated WWF matches ever.

WWF World champion Hogan was at the height of his popularity, while Andre had traded in his reputation as the gentle giant and become a rulebreaker.

A North American record live crowd of 93,173 was on hand at the Silverdome in Pontiac, Michigan, for the event.

The "Hulkster" retained his title when he legdropped Andre and pinned him for the win at the 12:01 mark. To this day, fans argue about what was most remarkable about the win, the fact that Hogan dealt Andre his first pinfall loss ever, or the fact that before the legdrop, the Hulkster actually managed to bodyslam the 525-pound behemoth!

RIC FLAIR vs. RICK STEAMBOAT (February 20, 1989)

This bout marked the first time in five years that these two consummate athletes had met in the ring. Steamboat and Flair had feuded on and off since the mid-1970s. Both men were in peak physical condition. In this bout, it was Flair's NWA World title that was on the line.

It was one of the all-time classic scientific wrestling encounters. With about 20 minutes gone in the match, Steamboat leaped off the top rope and onto the "Nature Boy." Flair accidentally crashed into referee Tommy Young. Steamboat covered Flair for the pin, but Young was too groggy to make the count. Flair managed to pin Steamboat, but again the pin went uncounted.

A second referee, Teddy Long, came to the ring. Flair went for his finishing move, the figure-four leglock. Steamboat reversed the hold and cradled Flair for the pin, which this time was counted. After 23:18 of pure wrestling action, a new NWA World champion was crowned.

SHAWN MICHAELS vs. BRET HART
(November 9, 1997)

Going into this bout in Montreal, Quebec, on November 9, 1997, WWF World champion Bret Hart had already declared his intentions to leave the WWF and enter WCW. WWF owner Vince McMahon had ordered Hart to throw the match, to lose on purpose. Hart had no desire to lose on purpose, especially in front of fans in his home country.

According to Hart, McMahon gave him his word that there would be no monkey business in the match. Three seconds after Michaels locked Hart in a sharpshooter, though, referee Earl Hebner—acting on orders from McMahon—called for the bell and declared that Hart had submitted. Hart, who clearly had never submitted, was enraged. He stormed back to the dressing room and, according to witnesses, punched McMahon several times.

Hart's frustration notwithstanding, he had lost in front of his "hometown" fans. Michaels was the new WWF World champion.

STING vs. HOLLYWOOD HOGAN
(December 28, 1997)

Wrestling seemed topsy-turvy at the end of 1997: Beloved WWF star Hulk Hogan had become despised WCW competitor and NWO (New World Order) leader "Hollywood" Hogan. Sting, one of the most popular and charismatic wrestlers in WCW history, had not wrestled for 16 months.

Though Sting hadn't wrestled, he had made his presence known in WCW rings. He developed a habit of appearing out of nowhere, descending into the middle of the ring during a match from high in the arena's rafters, and dispensing his own brand of justice with a baseball bat. Through it all, Sting continued to declare that he wanted Hogan. For his part, Hogan wanted no part of the "Stinger." Nevertheless, WCW promoters scheduled Sting's world title bout for December 28, 1997, at the Starrcade pay-per-view event. As champion, Hogan had little choice but to follow their orders.

Hogan was confident as he entered the ring. After all, Sting hadn't wrestled in a year and a half. Hogan's physical assault was relentless, but when he tried to pin Sting, something went wrong. There was no bell signaling the end of the match. Bret Hart had appeared at ringside and prevented the bell from ringing. Hart, who held a referee's license that night, restarted the match. Sting was energized and came back to defeat Hogan by submission. Sting was the new WCW World champion.

SHAWN MICHAELS vs. STEVE AUSTIN (March 29, 1998)

"Stone Cold" Steve Austin had the opportunity to wrestle WWF World champion Shawn Michaels at WrestleMania XIV, and he made the most of it, despite his escalating war with WWF owner Vince McMahon.

McMahon, along with a sellout crowd in Boston, Massachusetts, watched with great anticipation as Austin and Michaels squared off, with boxing superstar Mike Tyson as special ringside "enforcer" referee. Things looked bad

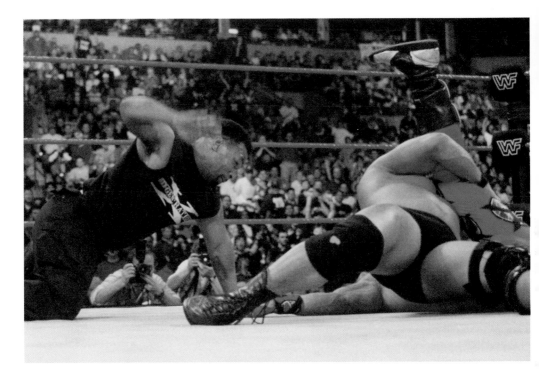

for Austin when Tyson showed up wearing a D-Generation X T-shirt, perhaps signaling Tyson's support of Michaels.

After WWF officials ordered D-Generation X members Chyna and Triple H back to the dressing room, Austin launched an amazing attack on Michaels, scoring four two-counts within 90 seconds. With 16 minutes gone, Michaels applied a figure-four leglock, but Austin reversed it into a figure-four of his own. Then Michaels clamped on a sleeperhold, but Austin backed his foe into the turnbuckle, knocking the referee unconscious.

Austin landed a "stone-cold stunner," covered Michaels, and waited for somebody to count the pinfall. To Michaels' amazement, Tyson bounded into the ring and made the three-count. Austin won his first WWF World

Boxer Mike Tyson, left, counts out WWF champion Shawn Michaels while Steve Austin holds him down for the pin. Tyson served as a "special enforcer" for their WWF championship match at Wrestle-Mania XIV on March 29, 1998.

title. The Stone Cold era of WWF wrestling had officially begun.

BILL GOLDBERG vs. HOLLYWOOD HOGAN (July 6, 1998)

Just weeks after a new era had begun in the WWF, another new era began in WCW, in front of more than 41,000 fans at the Georgia Dome in Atlanta.

Goldberg was just a rookie on July 6, 1998, when he defeated the seemingly invincible Hogan during a Nitro *broadcast, and became the new WCW World champion.*

Coming into the match, Hollywood Hogan was the WCW World champion, and Goldberg was the undefeated rookie sensation.

The match took place during a live broadcast of WCW *Monday Nitro*, and more than five million U.S. homes were tuned in to see Goldberg (who had defeated Scott Hall earlier in the evening to secure the title match) battle Hogan for the world title.

The match was an awesome display of wrestling power, and Goldberg's attack was relentless. Along the way, Goldberg recovered from three Hogan legdrops, then obliterated Hogan with a spear and a jackhammer to score the pinfall victory and capture the title.

Just as Hogan had devastated the Iron Sheik 14 years earlier to herald the arrival of Hulkamania, Goldberg had taken the mantle of Hulkamania and started a new era of his own.

KEVIN NASH vs. BILL GOLDBERG
(December 27, 1998)

Starrcade '98 was a memorable night in Washington, D.C., as fans in the nation's capital saw Nash win his first WCW World title in a match drenched in controversy.

After several minutes of furious action, Nash was on the mat and about to get pinned by Goldberg when Disco Inferno ran into the ring. Goldberg disposed of Inferno, then disposed of another interfering star, Bam Bam Bigelow. Goldberg, who had never lost a match in his career, turned his attention back to Nash. At about that time, Nash's friend, Scott Hall, walked to ringside dressed as a security guard. Hall grabbed Goldberg, shoved an electric cattle prod into his chest, and administered a current that sent Goldberg convulsing to the mat, where he was easily pinned by Nash.

Not only was Nash the new WCW World champion, but he had become only the fifth wrestler ever to hold both the WWF and WCW World titles. The match marked Goldberg's first ever professional loss and signaled that the Outsiders—the rulebreaking team of Hall and Nash—were together again.

3 GREAT CHAMPIONSHIP MATCHES

World titles aren't the only singles championships that inspire wrestlers to levels of greatness. Many of the sport's top stars have had their most shining moments battling for championships like the WWF Intercontinental title, the NWA and WCW U.S. heavyweight championships, and the Extreme Championship Wrestling (ECW) heavyweight title.

Though these titles are sometimes referred to as secondary championships, there is nothing secondary about the respect that the champions command. The action surrounding these titles is as brutal, intense, and memorable as that involving the world titles in the sport. Here are some of the greatest championship matches from 1983 to 1999.

GREG VALENTINE vs. RODDY PIPER
(April 30, 1983)

The era of pay-per-view wrestling was still years away, but this U.S. heavyweight title bout would have been a main event had pay-per-view been available.

Roddy Piper was the champion coming into the match, having defeated Greg Valentine just two weeks earlier in the same arena in Greensboro, North Carolina. The level of ani-

---

Whether battling Hulk Hogan, Kevin Nash, or Sid Vicious, Bill Goldberg has had his share of memorable matches.

mosity between the two men was about as high as it could possibly be. As a result, the match was one of the most brutal confrontations ever witnessed by Mid-Atlantic wrestling fans.

Greg "the Hammer" Valentine grabbed the U.S. championship belt off a table at ringside and proceeded to bash "Rowdy" Roddy Piper in the head with it again and again. Blood began pouring down Piper's head, and Valentine continued his brutal assault.

Sandy Scott, an NWA official stationed at ringside, ran into the ring and examined Piper. His ear had been ripped apart so badly, Scott was compelled to stop the match on the spot and award the bout and the belt to Valentine. Piper suffered permanent hearing loss, but the feud was far from over, as the two would meet in another great bout, at Starrcade '83 (see chapter 6).

RICK STEAMBOAT vs. RANDY SAVAGE (March 29, 1987)

For some, this match was overshadowed by the WWF World title bout between Hulk Hogan and Andre the Giant (see chapter 2). For many fans, however, this WWF Intercontinental title match was the best match at WrestleMania III, which was arguably the best WrestleMania of them all.

Savage came in to the bout with the belt, but Steamboat came to the ring with a grudge. During a previous title match, Savage had injured Steamboat's esophagus by ramming it with a timekeeper's bell. Steamboat wasn't just after the title, he was out for revenge, and he had more than 93,000 fans on hand cheering him on at the Silverdome in Pontiac, Michigan.

The bout was 14 minutes and 35 seconds of pure action. Most of the contest took place either above the mat or out of the ring on the arena floor. There were an astonishing 19 two-counts in the match—an average of one every 46 seconds! The end of the match saw Savage grab the bell and climb to the top rope in another attempt to injure Steamboat. George "the Animal" Steele pushed Savage off the top

Ricky Steamboat prepares to leap off of the top rope onto Randy "Macho Man" Savage below during their WrestleMania II match on March 29, 1987.

rope, and Steamboat rolled Savage up for the pinfall victory and the WWF Intercontinental title.

BRET HART vs. CURT HENNIG
(August 26, 1991)

In 1991, Bret Hart was undergoing a remarkable transformation. Known worldwide as one of the best tag team wrestlers ever (the Hart Foundation—Bret Hart and Jim Neidhardt—had two WWF World tag team titles to their credit), "the Hitman" was in the midst of becoming one of the world's best known solo stars.

This SummerSlam pay-per-view match in New York's Madison Square Garden cemented Hart's singles status. It marked the first major singles title that Hart would win, though many more would follow, including five WWF World titles and two WCW World titles.

It also marked the end of Curt Hennig's wrestling career. The back injury that had been plaguing "Mr. Perfect" for months was exacerbated by Hart's sharpshooter—a version of the scorpion deathlock, a leglock that places excruciating pressure on the victim's thighs and lower back. Hart caused Hennig to submit at the 18-minute-and-4-second mark, giving him the WWF Intercontinental title.

RAZOR RAMON vs. SHAWN MICHAELS
(March 20, 1994)

Pro Wrestling Illustrated magazine called this "one of the greatest matches of all time" and named it match of the year for 1994.

The intercontinental title had been in dispute for many months. Michaels won the title

Despite bringing the ladder down on Razor, Michaels was unable to defeat him at WrestleMania X in 1994. But his fans didn't mind; they loved every minute of the heart-stopping action in the Michaels/Ramon feud.

on June 6, 1993, but was stripped of the belt by the WWF for failing to meet certain contractual obligations. Ramon won the title on September 27, 1993, by defeating Rick Martel (the two were the last men left in a 20-man battle royal to determine the top contenders to the belt), but Michaels refused to accept the WWF's sanctioning of Ramon's championship. The WrestleMania X ladder match was intended to settle the dispute once and for all.

One paragraph of description cannot do the match justice: Ramon climbed to the top of the ladder to claim victory, but the match had been 18 minutes and 45 seconds of pure heart-stopping action. At one point, Michaels folded up the ladder, brought it to a corner, climbed to the top rope, and fell—with the ladder!—onto Ramon. At another point, Michaels climbed to the top of the ladder nearly 15 feet above the ring and dove from the top onto Ramon.

Anyone who saw this match will not soon forget it.

REY MISTERIO JR. vs. DEAN MALENKO
(July 8, 1996)

There are many titles in WCW: the world title, the world tag team title, the U.S. heavyweight title, and the television championship.

On July 8, 1996, the WCW cruiserweight title (which had been revived on March 20, 1996, when Shinjiri Otani defeated Chris Benoit in Nagoya, Japan) took its place among WCW's other championships and demanded to be noticed.

The bout took place on a broadcast of WCW *Monday Nitro*, Malenko had held the title just two months and six days when he stepped into the ring in Orlando, Florida, but Misterio was not to be denied, and the California native with a track record of success in Mexico succeeded in capturing his first major American championship. With this exciting match, interest in the cruiserweight division of WCW was reborn.

TERRY FUNK vs. RAVEN
(April 13, 1997)

Extreme Championship Wrestling (ECW) grew out of a regional organization formed in 1992 and known as Eastern Championship Wrestling. ECW gained a small but incredibly devoted following by staging cards featuring ultraviolent matches. In 1997, ECW expanded into the world of pay-per-view wrestling.

"Barely Legal" on April 13 in Philadelphia was ECW's first-ever pay-per-view show, and the main event saw ECW heavyweight champion Raven defending his title against wrestling veteran Terry Funk.

The bout was an incredible bloodbath. Perhaps more remarkable, though, was the fact that Funk, a former NWA World champion, was, at 53 years old, nearly two decades older than Raven. Funk's experience and enthusiasm carried him to an ECW title victory, beginning a violent title reign that lasted nearly four months.

BOOKER T vs. CHRIS BENOIT
(May 3, 1998)

What an amazing week it was in WCW: On April 30, 1998, Chris Benoit captured the federation's television championship from Booker T in Augusta, Georgia. On May 1, Booker regained the title in Greenville, South Carolina. On May 2, Benoit regained the title in North Charleston, South Carolina. On May 3, Booker regained the title in Savannah, Georgia. On May 4, Dave Finlay captured the WCW Television title from Booker.

The level of competitive energy surrounding the television title was unlike anything professional wrestling has ever seen. Five title changes in five days is unprecedented for any championship, much less a major title in a major federation.

The May 3 bout was the best of the bunch, the wrestling equivalent of a tennis match that just seems to go on and on for hours before one or the other of the evenly matched competitors scores.

D-LO BROWN vs. JEFF JARRETT
(July 27, 1999)

D-Lo Brown came into the match holding a European championship. Jarrett came into the bout holding the WWF Intercontinental title. Brown left the ring in Dayton, Ohio, with both belts, accomplishing one of the rarest feats in professional wrestling: simultaneous dual championships. It barely mattered that Brown had used one of the belts to smash Jarrett in the head and score the pin.

It was a doubly amazing accomplishment, considering the fact that just two years earlier, Brown wasn't even a wrestler. He was serving as a bodyguard in Faaroq's Nation of Domination clique in the WWF.

Brown's stint as a double champion lasted only until SummerSlam 1999 on August 22, though his feud with Jarrett continued for many months thereafter.

CHYNA vs. JEFF JARRETT
(October 17, 1999)

At a height of 5' 9" and a weight of 201 pounds, Chyna, the most amazing female wrestler in the WWF, seemed to be evenly matched with Jeff Jarrett, who stood 5' 10" and weighed 230. But in terms of pure muscle, Chyna was physically fit in a way that Jarrett could never hope to be.

At the WWF's "No Mercy" pay-per-view card, Jarrett had no chance. He was humbled in a surprisingly violent contest by Chyna, who smashed male chauvinist Jarrett in the head with his own guitar, then pinned him and cemented her place in the wrestling record books by becoming the first woman in the history of the sport to hold the WWF Intercontinental title, a major men's title. Her reign lasted nearly two months, and before the year 2000 was through, she had captured the title twice more.

BILL GOLDBERG vs. SID VICIOUS (October 24, 1999)

Las Vegas was the location of WCW's Halloween Havoc pay-per-view card in 1999, and Goldberg was the man everybody was watching.

Absent from competition for much of the year following a staggeringly successful 1998, Goldberg was an unknown quantity coming into the bout. Would the ankle and knee injury he suffered in a May 9 match with Sting still trouble him?

The answer was a resounding "no." Goldberg was far more vicious than Vicious, whose U.S. title reign was cut short at one month and 12 days when the referee was forced to halt the brutal contest due to excessive bleeding on the part of the champion.

GREAT GRUDGE MATCHES

A grudge match is something special. While titles may be on the line in grudge matches, in most cases those championships are irrelevant. In fact, winning or losing often becomes irrelevant. What matters most to the participants in these bouts is exacting revenge on one's opponent, inflicting as much damage as humanly (and sometimes inhumanly) possible, and being willing to absorb incredible amounts of punishment, so long as one's opponent absorbs more. In grudge matches, sportsmanship takes a back seat to the obsession of wanting to do away with one's enemy once and for all

Grudge matches are the kinds of matches that cause the pulse of a wrestling federation to race. They involve participants who will do anything to win. They are among the most brutal and violent spectacles in the sport.

BRUNO SAMMARTINO vs. LARRY ZBYSZKO
(August 9, 1980)

Bruno Sammartino was WWF World champion for most of the '60s and a good chunk of the '70s. He was a hero to millions, including a young wrestler named Larry Zbyszko, who was fortunate enough to call Sammartino his mentor.

Mankind backs the Rock into the corner of the ring and prepares to deliver his mandible claw maneuver.

Zbyszko's ambition, however, would get in the way of his good sense. In 1980 the student turned against his teacher. Zbyszko split Sammartino's head wide open with a chair. Disgraceful insults that could never be taken back were hurled with abandon.

Zbyszko quickly became one of the most hated wrestlers in the history of the WWF.

On a hot summer evening on August 9, 1980, in New York's Shea Stadium, Sammartino and Zbyszko entered a steel cage as nearly 41,000 fans watched and hoped that "The Living Legend" would claim victory by being the first to leave the cage.

The bout was short on style but long on violence. Zbyszko nearly escaped the cage twice, but each time Sammartino dragged his student back into the ring to administer more punishment. At 4 seconds past the 14-minute mark, the fans' collective hopes were realized as Sammartino left the cage, claimed victory, and avenged the wrongs that had been done to him by his faithless protege.

JERRY LAWLER vs. ANDY KAUFMAN (April 5, 1982)

This match marked the first time that the late comedian Andy Kaufman, who declared himself the "Intergender Wrestling Champion" because he repeatedly wrestled and defeated women, wrestled another man.

Kaufman won national fame as a star of the popular television show Taxi. Jerry "the King" Lawler was a mat legend in his home city of Memphis, Tennessee. For many long weeks, Kaufman had been sending videotaped insults to Memphis, degrading the fans and insulting

Jerry "the King" Lawler's infamous match with the late comedian Andy Kaufman was later immortalized in the 1999 film Man on the Moon, *about Kaufman's life.*

the wrestlers. Lawler decided the time had come to defend his home turf. The match was signed, and Kaufman traveled to Memphis to meet Lawler in his home ring.

After a lot of stalling on Kaufman's part, the match was no match at all: A piledriver by the King 6 minutes and 50 seconds into the event resulted in Lawler's disqualification (the pile-driver was then an illegal maneuver in Memphis). After the bell rang, Lawler gave a limp Kaufman another piledriver.

When Lawler and Kaufman appeared together on David Letterman's talk show on

July 28, 1982, Kaufman was still wearing a neck brace. It didn't matter to Lawler, who was still outraged by Kaufman's arrogance and insults. Lawler slapped the comedian out of his chair as Letterman looked on in shock. The match, along with the events before and after the confrontation, remains one of the highlights of both Lawler and Kaufman's careers.

RODDY PIPER & PAUL ORNDORFF vs. HULK HOGAN & MR. T (March 31, 1985)

It was an amazing year in the WWF. The "rock 'n' wrestling connection" was in full swing. Hulk Hogan was the sport's hottest star. Roddy Piper insulted rock stars like Cyndi Lauper, who were attracted to the WWF, and he put down Hulk Hogan, who wore the championship belt he desired.

On February 18, 1985, Piper and Hogan battled in "The War To Settle The Score," broadcast live on MTV. The bout ended in a disqualification when Lauper and actor Mr. T interfered. Next stop: New York's Madison Square Garden and the first WrestleMania.

Hogan and T joined forces. Piper called on his friend, "Mr. Wonderful" Paul Orndorff. The stage was set for the most widely viewed (up to that time) grudge match in history. The first WrestleMania, packed with celebrities like rock star Cyndi Lauper, the famous pianist Liberace, and boxer Muhammad Ali, was made available to 135 closed-circuit television locations and drew an estimated viewership of 400,000. Hogan and Mr. T won when the Hulkster pinned Orndorff.

HULK HOGAN vs. KING KONG BUNDY
(April 7, 1986)

This match actually began months earlier when King Kong Bundy interfered in a match between Hulk Hogan and Don Muraco in Phoenix, Arizona. Bundy used the full force of his 446 pounds to deliver a series of "big splash" maneuvers, in which he essentially sits down on his opponent at high speed. Hogan suffered a cerebral concussion, plus multiple injuries to his lower back, ribs, and neck and spine area.

When the WrestleMania II main event steel cage match was signed for seven weeks later, many actually counted Hogan as the underdog. They believed his injuries weren't fully healed.

Hogan entered the match with his ribs still taped. Bundy started the match by pulling off the bandages and using them to choke the Hulkster. Hogan retaliated by slamming Bundy's head into the cage and opening up a bloody gash. Hogan retained his WWF World title by being the first man to climb over the top of the cage.

THE ROCK 'N' ROLL EXPRESS vs.
THE MIDNIGHT EXPRESS
(November 26, 1987)

The Midnight Express, managed by Jim Cornette, originally consisted of Dennis Condrey and Bobby Eaton. In August 1986, they lost the NWA World tag team belts to the Rock 'n' Roll Express. Cornette replaced Condrey with Stan Lane, and in 1987 the Midnights captured the U.S. tag team title.

They spent most of the year feuding with the Rock 'n' Rolls—Rick Morton and Robert

Gibson—in a war that amazed fans with its high-speed intensity.

The teams' scaffold match at Starrcade '87 was anything but a high-speed contest, but it was a classic grudge bout. The four men competed high above the ring in a bout in which the object was to push both members of the other team off the scaffold.

Rick Morton managed to grab Cornette's tennis racket and bring it with him up the scaffold. Eaton threw a blinding white powder in both his opponents' faces, but it was his own partner, Lane, who first fell to the canvas 20 feet below. Left to a two-on-one disadvantage, Eaton was driven off the scaffold, leaving Morton and Gibson the victors in a bout that was undoubtedly as terrifying for the participants as it was for the fans watching them.

RIC FLAIR vs. TERRY FUNK
(November 15, 1989)

On May 7, 1989, Ric Flair captured the NWA World title from Rick Steamboat in a match that had several ringside judges. One of those judges was Terry Funk, who shook Flair's hand in congratulations, then promptly piledrived him through a ringside table.

At the Great American Bash on July 23, Funk tried to smother Flair by suffocating him with a plastic bag wrapped around his head, but Flair pinned Funk to retain his world title.

At Clash of the Champions IX on November 15, broadcast live on SuperStation TBS, Flair and Funk met in a match that was the culmination of their feud. The winner was the man who could make his opponent say, "I quit"; the loser would have to retire. The match was 18 minutes and 33 seconds of agonizing action that spilled in and out of the ring and saw each man gain painful advantage over the other. In the end, though, it was Funk who uttered the fateful words, after which both men shook hands in a show of respect that won a standing ovation from the crowd.

LEX LUGER vs. YOKOZUNA
(July 4, 1993)

Hulk Hogan had left the WWF to make movies and television shows in Hollywood,

A huge crowd gathered at Madison Square Garden in New York to watch WWF champion Yokozuna battle Lex Luger at WrestleMania X.

leaving the federation without a savior. Lex Luger tried to fill the void.

Former Sumo wrestler Yokozuna had defeated Hogan for the WWF World title on June 13. On July 4, the WWF held "The Stars and Stripes Challenge." Yokozuna had the title Luger coveted, and Luger wanted to gain the support of the fans.

On the occasion of the nation's most patriotic holiday, Yokozuna made a challenge to wrestlers everywhere: he would be on the deck of the U.S.S. *Intrepid* aircraft carrier in New York City, and anyone was invited to try to bodyslam him. Many tried, including Scott Steiner, Bob Backlund, and Randy Savage. All failed. In the July 4 battle of Yokozuna vs. the U.S., the U.S. was declared the loser.

Then Luger arrived at the challenge via helicopter, climbed into the ring, and accomplished the impossible: He bodyslammed the 568-pound WWF World champion! Though he never dethroned the big man for the belt, Luger was nonetheless an American hero.

BRET HART vs. OWEN HART
(March 20, 1994)

It was the brother vs. brother feud that destroyed the hearts of Helen and Stu Hart, the parents of Bret and Owen, and saw the two competitors battle in dozens of arenas worldwide. Owen was jealous of Bret's success, and couldn't contain his rage. Owen attacked his sibling at the Royal Rumble, on January 22, 1994, but the most memorable match of this feud came at WrestleMania X.

Appropriate to the skills of both men, the match was an intense but scientific affair, with each displaying excellent skills to match their fiery determination. The bout ended when Bret, atop his brother's shoulders, tried to bring his own body over and roll Owen up for the pin. Owen caught Bret's legs, and rolled him up for the pin at the 20:21 mark. It was the only time in the feud that Owen scored a clean win over his brother, and he did so during the most important WWF card of the year.

Brothers Bret and Owen Hart, who first learned to wrestle from their father, Stu Hart, showcased their skills with an intense match at Wrestlemania X that saw Owen emerge as the winner.

Incredibly, Bret bounced back from the loss to wrestle again later in the card and capture the WWF World title from Yokozuna.

THE ROCK vs. MANKIND (January 24, 1999)

Like the famous Ric Flair vs. Terry Funk match a decade earlier, this was an "I Quit" match. The man who made the other say "I quit" first would leave the ring with the WWF World title.

Mankind was the champion coming in to this Royal Rumble main event, while the Rock was loyal to WWF owner Vince McMahon, and the top star in McMahon's Team Corporate stable of competitors. The match spilled out of the ring and all through Arrowhead Pond arena in Anaheim, California. The fierce competitors used foreign objects like the ringside bell, the announcer's microphone, and a ladder in their attempt to make the other submit.

The war between Vince McMahon and Steve Austin heated up the ratings for the WWF.

The Rock hit Mankind in the head with a chair not just once, but 10 times! And when Mankind was heard to say "I quit," the Rock became the WWF World champion. It was later

discovered that McMahon and his associates had previously taped Mankind saying those words, and played the tape at the appropriate moment in the match.

Mankind got his revenge two days later, when he regained the title in a falls-count-any-where match taped in an empty arena and broadcast during halftime of the Super Bowl.

VINCE MCMAHON vs. STEVE AUSTIN (February 14, 1999)

There was no title at stake in the match, simply the number-one contender's spot for the WWF World title. Vince McMahon, owner of the WWF, wanted to keep the title away from "Stone Cold" Steve Austin and was willing to put his body on the line to do it.

Appropriately, the match headlined the "St. Valentine's Day Massacre" pay-per-view card. It was indeed a massacre, a war inside a steel cage that saw Austin choke his boss with a TV cable before the match even officially began, and push him off the outside of the cage onto a ringside announcers' table. When paramedics tried to wheel McMahon away on a stretcher, Austin continued the attack.

McMahon suffered multiple injuries, including a broken tailbone, and he lost the match when Austin was inadvertently flung through the cage door as former WCW World champion Paul Wight cut through the canvas and made his way into the ring for his WWF debut. The winner of a cage match is the person who first exits the cage through the door. Even though Austin was inadvertently hurled through the door, he did win the match by the rules.

5 GREAT TAG TEAM MATCHES

They're twice as powerful, twice as volatile, twice as determined, and twice as capable of producing greatness in any given match on any given night. Wrestling's world tag team titles are as prestigious as the singles titles in their respective federations. They represent a level of excellence that everyone strives for, but only few achieve. Over the years, there have been dozens of great tag teams, collectively participating in hundreds of great tag team matches. Here are just a few of the very best.

THE ROAD WARRIORS vs. IVAN & NIKITA KOLOFF (April 18, 1985)

In 1985, the Road Warriors were to tag team wrestling what Hulk Hogan was to singles wrestling: powerful, charismatic, and dominant.

Russian powerhouse Nikita Koloff and his uncle, former WWF World champion Ivan Koloff, sought to challenge that dominance. At the time, the Koloffs held the NWA World tag team title, while the Warriors were tag team champions of the now-defunct AWA.

This match, held in Washington, D.C., was notable in that it was a rare cross-federation meeting of two world championship

Road Warriors Animal and Hawk burst onto the WWF tag team scene in the 1980s and quickly dominated the competition.

teams. An awesome exhibition of wrestling brutality and a virtual clinic in power wrestling, the brutal contest saw the Warriors and the Koloffs battle to a double-disqualification.

THE SHEEPHERDERS vs. THE FANTASTICS (June 14, 1986)

Years before ECW took wrestling to the extreme, the Universal Wrestling Federation (UWF) was bringing new heights of violence to the mat sport. In 1986, the top two teams in the UWF were the Sheepherders (later known as the Bushwhackers in the WWF) and the Fantastics, Bobby Fulton and Tommy Rogers.

Nobody imagined that fan favorites Fulton and Rogers could sink to depraved depths of violence, but that's the effect that the Sheepherders, Butch Miller and Luke Williams, had on them. When promoters put these warring teams into a ring surrounded by barbed wire, the result was a sickening display of violence and gore, and a quartet of hideously bloody competitors. By the time it was all over, both teams looked as if they had been mauled by wild animals.

THE BRITISH BULLDOGS vs. THE HART FOUNDATION (January 26, 1987)

On January 26, 1987, the Hart Foundation captured the WWF World tag team title from the British Bulldogs in Tampa, Florida.

That may sound like just another entry in a long list of WWF World tag team title changes, but it doesn't begin to hint at the excellence displayed in this match. The Bulldogs—Davey Boy Smith and Dynamite Kid—are viewed by

Hart Foundation members Jim Neidhart and Bret Hart receive the WWF World tag team belts after their victory over the British Bulldogs.

many wrestling experts as the most acrobatic tag team ever. The Harts—Bret Hart and Jim Neidhardt—were spectacular as well.

Placing the two teams in a ring was a wide-open invitation for all fans present to hang their jaws open in sheer awe at the athleticism both on the mat and in the air. Adding the WWF World title into the mix only propelled their skills to a higher level.

STING & LEX LUGER vs. RICK & SCOTT STEINER (May 19, 1991)

Wrestling is a sport in which friend wrestles friend only when one of those friends has turned against the other. Well, usually. In this incredible match, four friends—each astoundingly popular in WCW at the time—assembled in the ring for an amazing display of wrestling intensity and mutual respect. The Steiners held the WCW World tag team title at the time, while Luger was U.S. heavyweight champion.

The match came to a disappointing end when Nikita Koloff interfered, smashed Sting in the face with a chain, and allowed Scott Steiner to score the pinfall he really did not want to accept. Readers of *Pro Wrestling Illustrated* magazine voted this bout Match of the Year.

RICK & SCOTT STEINER vs. TED DIBIASE & IRWIN R. SCHYSTER (June 14, 1993)

When Rick and Scott Steiner left WCW to compete in the WWF, fans were stunned. The Steiners were three-time NWA/WCW World tag team champions who embraced pure wrestling action in a way that the more cartoonish WWF stars usually didn't. The obvious question was raised often: Could Rick and Scott make it in the very different world of the WWF? This match in Columbus, Ohio, answered that question with a resounding yes. Rick and Scott exhibited the kind of high-impact style of wrestling seldom seen in the WWF at that time, and they did so with notable success. Their victory in this match ended a formidable eight-month title reign by DiBiase and Schyster—and began the first of what would be two WWF World tag team title reigns for the Steiners.

THE NASTY BOYS vs. HARLEM HEAT (May 21, 1995)

Many wrestling commentators called it a "Slamboree slugfest" when Nasty Boys Jerry Sags and Brian Knobs pummeled Harlem Heat—Booker T and Stevie Ray—on the way to a WCW World tag team title victory at WCW's

Slamboree pay-per-view card. It was a battle of signature maneuvers: Heat's powerful legdrops vs. the Nastys' stunning piledrivers.

Incredibly, Sags fought most of the match on his own, as Knobs was injured before the bout. Even so, the battle was remarkably even, and came to a championship-change finish when Sags delivered an elbowsmash from the top rope to Booker T, then rolled him up for the pin to begin the Nastys' third NWA/WCW World title reign.

TEAM NWO vs. TEAM WCW vs. TEAM PIPER
(March 16, 1997)

WCW was under siege. The NWO—the New World Order—had declared war, and with a battalion of brawn that included Hulk Hogan, Kevin Nash, Scott Hall, and Randy Savage, they seemed to have victory close at hand.

WCW responded with an army of their own: the Giant, Lex Luger, Rick Steiner, and Scott Steiner. The two armies met in a War Games match that saw them joined by a third quartet of grapplers, Team Piper: Roddy Piper, Jeff Jarrett, Chris Benoit, and Steve McMichael.

Hogan pinned Luger in the match, giving the NWO a significant victory. They earned the right to demand a title match for any WCW championship anytime they wanted one.

STEVE AUSTIN & SHAWN MICHAELS vs. OWEN HART & DAVEY BOY SMITH
(May 25, 1997)

Though both Austin and Michaels initially gained fame as tag team wrestlers—Austin as a member of the Hollywood Blonds with Brian

Pillman, Michaels as a member of the Midnight Rockers with Marty Jannetty—by May 1997, both had firmly established themselves as singles stars. Michaels had two WWF World and three WWF Intercontinental titles to his credit, while Austin, a former WCW U.S. heavyweight champion, was on the verge of WWF solo superstardom.

So it was a remarkable occasion that these two singles powerhouses would reach back to their respective tag team pasts to join forces. Their target was the WWF World tag team title, and the fact that each man could place his singles ambitions aside for the good of their team was a testament to their emotional maturity and wrestling versatility. Their tag team skills rose to the occasion in Evansville, Indiana, as they dethroned the superb tag team champions, Hart and Smith. The Austin-Michaels reign was short-lived, though. On June 9 Michaels walked out of the WWF, and the title was declared vacant.

HARLEM HEAT vs. BILLY KIDMAN & KONNAN vs. BRIAN KNOBS & HUGH MORRIS
(October 24, 1999)

The main event of Halloween Havoc in 1999 was this incredible three-way match to determine the WCW World tag team championship.

The wild action was all over the arena in this astounding "street fight rules" match that lasted only 5:05, but had enough intensity to fill a bout 10 times as long. It didn't take long for several tables and trash cans to be completely destroyed as they were used as weapons against various competitors.

In the ring, Hugh Morris smashed Konnan through a table, enabling Kidman to subsequently score a pin. In the backstage area, meanwhile, Harlem Heat was double-teaming Brian Knobs, resulting in Booker T scoring the pin on Knobs at precisely the same time as Kidman scored his pin in the ring.

WCW officials determined that Booker's pinfall occurred first, and so Harlem Heat won their unprecedented 10th WCW World tag team championship.

THE DUDLEYS vs. THE HARDYS vs. EDGE & CHRISTIAN
(April 2, 2000)

This WrestleMania 2000 triangle match saw WWF World tag team champions the Dudleys defend against two other tag teams simultaneously! The belts were dangled high above the ring, and any wrestler who could climb a ladder and retrieve them would win the title for his team.

All six men seemed more intent on destroying their opponents than retrieving the belts. At one incredible point in the match, Jeff Hardy dove off the top of a 25-foot metal ladder, somersaulted through the air onto Buh-Buh Ray Dudley, who was lying prone on a table, and drove his body into the concrete floor below.

When the violence finally came to an end at the 22:35 mark, the Dudleys had proven their toughness, but Christian and Edge had climbed the ladder and retrieved the belts to become the new WWF World tag team champions.

GREAT SPECIALTY MATCHES

Wrestling at its most fundamental is the purest of sports: one competitor against another, armed with nothing but skills and wits. Yet pro wrestling in the last several decades has become far more than just sport. It's become an arena for settling grudges and a source of entertainment that demands its participants continue to find new ways to engage, and sometimes shock, the fans.

The following specialty matches show how the sport has figured out new ways to amaze the fans and stretch the skills of the athletes to their very limits.

BOB BACKLUND vs. JIMMY SNUKA
(Cage Match: June 28, 1982)

In the early 1980s, a cage match was a genuine specialty match, not the relatively common site it became by 2000. In the WWF of 1982, a cage match was a last resort.

Bob Backlund was the WWF World champion at the time, and he had already been defending his title against Jimmy "Superfly" Snuka for two months. Snuka wouldn't give up the challenge, though. It was time for the last resort.

This bout took place in New York's legendary Madison Square Garden and became a wrestling legend. Snuka, famous

---

Bob Backlund was the WWF's reigning champion in the early 1980s and managed to go undefeated for four straight years.

for his flying dives off the top turnbuckle, amazed the audience by scaling to the top turnbuckle—then continuing to the top of the cage itself. The crowd was breathless as Snuka spread his arms wide and launched himself into the air . . . only to miss Backlund, who staggered out of the cage and retained his title. Snuka didn't win the belt that night, but in setting a new standard for fearlessness in the sport, he won his rightful place in wrestling history.

RODDY PIPER vs. GREG VALENTINE (Dog Collar Chain Match: November 24, 1983)

Before there was WrestleMania, there was Starrcade, and in some ways Starrcade '83 was the best of them all. Though not a main event match, the dog collar chain match between Roddy Piper and Greg Valentine will forever be remembered as a Starrcade classic. Piper had suffered a severe ear injury at the hands of Valentine on April 30, 1983 (see chapter 3). Coming into this bout, Valentine continued to hold the U.S. title he won from Piper that night, but the title was not on the line. This was a match purely about revenge.

Each man wore a leather dog collar around his neck, and the collars were connected by a steel chain. Of course, each man was able to use the chain as a weapon, and neither man was able to escape the other, due to the chain that connected them.

Piper ultimately won the bout, gaining his revenge against Valentine, who nonetheless continued to reign as U.S. champion before losing the title to Dick Slater about three weeks later.

THE ROAD WARRIORS vs.
THE MIDNIGHT EXPRESS
(Scaffold Match: November 28, 1986)

There have been very few scaffold matches in pro wrestling, for good reason: They are extremely dangerous. A scaffold is constructed that allows the participants to compete on a narrow and precarious battleground 20 or 25 feet above the ring.

As the Warriors and the Midnights scaled to the top of the scaffold, the Starrcade crowd in Greensboro, North Carolina, was breathless: It appeared as if the scaffold would collapse at any moment.

The Express threw blinding powder in the eyes of the Warriors, but it didn't help their cause much. Eventually, both teams wound up hanging from the bottom of the scaffold kicking each other. Road Warriors Hawk and Animal won this war of attrition and, as Midnights Dennis Condrey and Bobby Eaton crashed to the mat below, they claimed victory.

After the match, the Warriors chased the other team's manager, Jim Cornette, to the top of the scaffold, then caused him to hang from below and fall to the canvas, sustaining a knee injury that plagued Cornette for years.

RIC FLAIR, SID VICIOUS, BARRY
WINDHAM, & LARRY ZBYSZKO vs. STING,
BRIAN PILLMAN, RICK & SCOTT STEINER
(War Games: February 24, 1991)

War Games was one of WCW's most popular contributions to the specialty match genre. In a War Games bout, two teams of four men battle inside a steel cage spanning two wrestling rings. The match starts with one man from each

At a three-ring Royal Rumble in 1996, the Giant, whose real name is Paul Wight, used his brawn to eliminate all of the other contenders and make himself the winner of the battle royal.

team, and every two minutes, a new competitor enters the cage. A pre-match coin toss determines which team will send the third man into the bout. The coin toss is crucial, since the team that wins the toss has a one-man advantage for three two-minute intervals (two on one, three on two, four on three) until all eight men have entered the ring.

This particular edition of War Games saw referee Nick Patrick stop the contest and award the victory to the team of Flair, Vicious,

Windham, and Zbyszko when Brian Pillman was rendered unconscious by two powerbombs delivered by Vicious.

60-MAN BATTLE ROYAL
(November 24, 1996)

Traditionally, a battle royal consists of 20 men in a ring, all battling at once. When a man is thrown over the top rope, he is eliminated. The last man standing is the victor. In 1996, at the World War III pay-per-view card, WCW took the concept further.

Three rings were set up, and there were 20 men in each ring. The prize for the last man standing was a title shot against WCW World champion Hulk Hogan.

The Giant, later known as both Paul Wight and the Big Show, used every inch of his 7' 4" height and every ounce of his 430 pounds to outlast the field and, in the end, hurl Kevin Nash and Lex Luger over the top rope simultaneously to be the last man standing. He won the title shot against Hogan, but was never able to capture the world championship belt from the Hulkster.

SHAWN MICHAELS vs. THE UNDERTAKER
(Casket Match: January 18, 1998)

What a gruesome concept: The winner is the first man to seal his opponent inside a casket.

For the Undertaker, who embraced all things death-related, the casket match was something of a specialty. In this Royal Rumble classic, however, after both men were in and out of the casket several times, Undertaker was defeated by WWF World champion Shawn Michaels after Undertaker's brother, Kane, interfered.

THE UNDERTAKER vs. MANKIND
(Hell in a Cell Match: June 28, 1998)

It's been said that in this bout, Mankind came as close to dying in the ring as anyone possibly can without actually dying.

Mankind entered the arena first, climbing to the roof of the steel cage with a steel chair in his hand. Undertaker followed Mankind to the top, and the two battled furiously until Undertaker threw Mankind off the top of the cage and through a broadcasters' table.

Doctors attended to Mankind, who scrambled off the stretcher that was wheeling him to the dressing room and climbed back to the top of the cage to battle Undertaker—who choke-slammed him through the roof of the cage!

The carnage continued. Undertaker slammed Mankind onto a bed of thumbtacks, then piledrived him for the win. Mankind sustained a dislocated shoulder, a bruised kidney, two cracked ribs, a concussion, several knocked-out teeth (including one tooth jammed through the top of his mouth and out his nostril), and hundreds of thumbtack holes in his skin.

Kids, do not try this at home.

ATSUSHI ONITA vs. MASA CHONO
(Electrified and Exploding Barbed Wire Match: April 10, 1999)

As if it's not enough to place two mortal enemies inside a wrestling ring surrounded with barbed wire instead of ropes, this match saw the barbed wire electrified and rigged to explode.

The Tokyo Dome was the host for this extreme battle of courage and determination, but the 63,000 fans on hand would not see a winner declared: The bout ended in a draw at the 16 minute and 10 second mark when both men were caught in the explosion and rendered unconscious.

THE GREAT MUTA vs. THE GREAT NITA
(No-rope, Barbed Wire, Barricade-mat, Electric-mine, Double-hell Death Match: August 28, 1999)

Exploding barbed-wire seemed like the ultimate extreme until this bit of sanctioned insanity.

International Wrestling Grand Prix (IWGP) champion the Great Muta defended his title against the Great Nita in front of 48,000 fans in

The Rock, Triple H, and the Giant argue during a fatal four-way match that also brought in Mankind. With help from the McMahon family, Triple H emerged as the winner.

Tokyo's Jinju Stadium. Barbed wire replaced the conventional ropes. The ring was littered with deadly electric mines. Both men fought for a large knife.

Muta scored the pinfall at the 13:32 mark after attacking Nita with the knife.

THE ROCK vs. BIG SHOW vs. MANKIND vs. TRIPLE-H (Fatal Four-way Match: April 2, 2000)

The "fatal four-way match" at WrestleMania 2000 was the most highly anticipated match of the year, a four-man elimination match with Triple-H's WWF World title on the line.

Each participant was accompanied by a member of the McMahon family: the Rock by WWF owner Vince McMahon; Mankind by

Stephanie McMahon kisses her husband Triple H. With Stephanie in his corner, Triple H had an edge over his opponents that helped him win the coveted WWF World title.

Vince's wife, Linda; Triple-H by their daughter, Stephanie; and Big Show by their son, Shane.

Late in the contest, the Rock and Triple-H were the only two men remaining. With over 26 minutes gone, Vince interfered on the Rock's behalf. Shane came to the ring and smashed Vince with a TV monitor. Vince and Shane battled as the Rock and Triple-H lay motionless in the ring. Bloodied, Vince was helped back to the locker room. The Rock got up and DDT'd Triple-H for a two-count. Shane got ready to hit the Rock with a chair, but the Rock slingshotted Triple-H into the chair. The Rock clobbered Triple-H and prepared to score the pin. Vince returned to the ring and nailed Shane. But then, Vince chaired the Rock. Triple-H covered the Rock for the pin at the 36:34 mark.

The Rock may have lost, but he emerged from the bout a bigger WWF hero than ever before.

Ask 50 wrestling fans to name the greatest match they've ever seen, and it's very possible you'll receive 50 different answers. It's likely that many of those matches are included in this book — but it's just as likely that many are not. Opinions over what constitutes a great match differ among wrestling fans.

Great matches occur at major pay-per-view events with worldwide acclaim, and in small promotions with little attention.

They all help make professional wrestling what it will continue to be for many decades to come: The greatest spectator sport in the world.

Chronology

1980   41,000 WWF fans cheer as Bruno Sammartino defeats his former student, Larry Zbyszko, in a steel cage match at New York's Shea Stadium on August 9

1982   Comedian Andy Kaufman wrestles Jerry "the King" Lawler on April 5

1983   Ric Flair defeats Harley Race on November 24 to capture the NWA World heavyweight championship. It is the first time the venerable title changes hands inside a steel cage

1984   Hulk Hogan defeats the Iron Sheik on January 23 to capture the WWF World title; Hulkamania is born

1985   In a rare title vs. title bout, NWA World tag team champions Ivan and Nikita Koloff battle AWA World tag team champions the Road Warriors to a double-disqualification in Washington, D.C., on April 18

1987   WrestleMania III draws 93,173 to the Silverdome in Pontiac, Michigan on March 29. In the main event, WWF World champion Hulk Hogan defeats and bodyslams Andre the Giant. In an incredible undercard match, Rick Steamboat captures the intercontinental title from Randy Savage

1998   Mankind sustains tremendous injuries while losing a "hell in a cell" match to the Undertaker on June 28

1999   Chyna defeats Jeff Jarrett for the WWF Intercontinental title on October 17, becoming the first woman in the history of pro wrestling to hold a major men's championship

Further Reading

Editors of London Publishing. *Inside Wrestling Presents Wrestling Supercards: WrestleMania! 14 Years of Wrestling Magic.* Fort Washington, Pennsylvania: London Publishing, 1999.

Editors of London Publishing. *Pro Wrestling Illustrated Presents The 2000 Wrestling Almanac and Book of Facts.* Fort Washington, Pennsylvania: London Publishing, 2000.

Editors of London Publishing. "PWI 10th Anniversary Book of Lists: The 50 Greatest Matches of the Past 10 Years." *Pro Wrestling Illustrated* (September 1989): 60–61.

Hunter, Matt. *Pro Wrestling's Greatest Tag Teams.* Philadelphia: Chelsea House Publishers, 2001.

Hunter, Matt. *Superstars of Men's Pro Wrestling.* Philadelphia: Chelsea House Publishers, 1998.

Ross, Dan. *Pro Wrestling's Greatest Wars.* Philadelphia: Chelsea House Publishers, 2001.

"Special Section: The Greatest Match I Ever Saw." *Wrestling Superstars* (August 2000): 17–37.

Index

Photo Credits
The Acci'Dent: p. 25; Associated Press/WWP: pp. 17, 40; Jeff Eisenberg Sports Photography: pp. 10, 18, 20, 23, 30, 33, 37, 39, 45, 54, 57, 58, 60; David Fitzgerald: pp. 6, 50; Howard Kernats Photography: pp. 2, 8, 42.

MATT HUNTER has spent nearly two decades writing about professional wrestling. In addition to this book on pro wrestling, the author's previously published volumes on the mat sport include *Jesse Ventura: The Story of the Wrestler They Call "The Body,"* *The Story of the Wrestler They Call "Hollywood" Hulk Hogan, Superstars of Pro Wrestling*, and *Wrestling Madness*. He has interviewed countless wrestlers on national television, photographed innumerable bouts from ringside, and written more magazine articles about the mat sport than he cares to calculate.